Original title:

A Heart Made of Snow

Copyright © 2024 Creative Arts Management OÜ

Author: Liam Sterling
ISBN HARDBACK: 978-9916-94-392-2
ISBN PAPERBACK: 978-9916-94-393-9

Snowbound Secrets

When snowflakes dance and twirl around,
They whisper secrets, funny and profound.
A carrot nose on a snowman grand,
Stealing mittens with icy hands.

In the yard, the snowball fights ensue,
Laughter echoes, oh what a view.
A slippery slope leads to a tumble,
With hot cocoa, we giggle and mumble.

Warmth Within the Chill

In winter's grip, I shiver and shake,
Yet snowman jokes are what we make.
Frosty smiles and frosty toes,
The warmth within, that nobody knows.

A hot chocolate's marshmallowy bliss,
In freezing temperatures, we can't resist.
We wrap up tight, in scarves we twist,
A frozen dance, we can't help but persist.

Traces of a Blushing Chill

Snowflakes flutter like tiny little spies,
They trickle down like well-cooked fries.
We stomp around, making footprints galore,
With icy surprises behind every door.

The cheeks turn red in winter's embrace,
As snowmen plot their snowy race.
We slip and slide, laughter rings true,
While whispers of snowflakes swish right through.

Memories in a Winter Wonderland

Snowmen grinning, hats askew,
Tripping over in our boots anew.
Whirling snowflakes, we chase and spin,
Making memories through thick and thin.

Snow forts built with childish glee,
A kingdom of laughter, just you and me.
Winter's canvas, all white and bright,
We chase the cold with pure delight.

Snowfall's Embrace

Frosty flakes dance in the air,
Wearing cozy mittens everywhere.
Snowmen grin with carrot noses,
While kids dive in, striking poses.

A blizzard's brew, hot cocoa delight,
Snowball fights turn laughter bright.
Umbrellas flipped, oh what a sight,
Winter's antics, pure delight!

Frozen in Time

Time stands still, as snowflakes swirl,
  Each one a unique little pearl.
  I slip and slide on icy ground,
Flailing limbs—a comedy abound.

Hot chocolate spills with every fall,
Giggles erupt, we laugh through it all.
  Frosty hats misplaced, what a mess,
  Immortalized in winter's dress.

The Glistening Silence

The world wears white in dazzling cheer,
Each step crunches, spreading good cheer.
Squirrels navigating in their gear,
Casually pondering 'what's the deal here?'

Snowflakes whisper secrets untold,
While joggers stumble, their stories bold.
The silence breaks—laughter rings out,
Winter's wonder, without a doubt!

Echoes of Snowflakes

They tumble down with giggles galore,
Covering rooftops, sidewalks, and more.
Chasing shadows, sleds zip down,
Laughter echoes, joy's the crown.

Snowballs fly like little missiles,
Dodging is key, oh what a bristle!
Lumpy snowmen, each one a bear,
Every face's a masterpiece rare!

Woven in Frost

In winter's chill, I find my glee,
A frosty dance, just me and me.
Snowflakes fall, a waltz divine,
Each one whispers, "I'm yours, don't whine!"

With mittens on, I trip and slide,
My snowman's got more charm than pride.
He leans to chat, his carrot nose,
I laugh and say, "You strike a pose!"

The icicles are my frozen friends,
They dangle low, but make no bends.
They glitter bright in the sun's bright glow,
"Watch me shine!" they seem to show.

A snowball fight ignites with flair,
I duck and dodge with frosty air.
Laughter rings, a merry sound,
In this white world, joy is found!

Breaths of Winter's Past

Old memories drift like cotton fluff,
Where icy whispers say, "That's tough!"
I recall the sled that wouldn't slide,
A bumpy ride, where fun's my guide.

The cozy nights by fireside glow,
With cocoa warm, I sip so slow.
But marshmallow fights erupt with glee,
My drink's a flood, oh woe is me!

Hats are floppy, scarves a mess,
In snowball teamwork, who feels the stress?
We aim so high, yet fall below,
Our wild hopes lost in winter's show.

Yet every puff of breath I see,
Transforms the air to poetry.
With every chuckle that the cold creates,
I find the warmth in frozen states!

Cold Currents

In winter's breath, I tried to cheer,
Laughter rang out, but no one could hear.
A snowball fight turned into a slip,
As I took a tumble, oh what a trip!

Bundled up tight, I braved the chill,
My nose was red, but I had the will.
With each frosty gust, I'd simply shout,
'Just call me a snowman, no doubt!'

The Dance of the Frost

The frost is dancing, wild and free,
Although my toes feel like they disagree.
I tried ballet on icy ground,
And now I'm the star of the slip-up sound!

With every twirl, I lose my grace,
I spin and land, oh what a face!
The snowflakes laugh as they settle down,
Beneath my flailing, clumsy crown.

Hidden Heat

I wrapped my scarf like a giant burrito,
In hopes to stay warm, but I'm still a mosquito.
The cocoa's hot, but I'm freezing here,
Just call me a snowman, I'm full of cheer!

I tried to warm up with a dance and a jig,
But my toes just laughed and wouldn't dig.
So here I sit with frosted feet,
In a winter wonderland, feeling quite neat!

Heart of the Frosted Night

Under the stars, I twirled with delight,
Only to trip on a snowdrift so white.
The moon just chuckled, what a sight to see,
A flurry of giggles enveloped me!

Sipping my cocoa, I grinned at the night,
While slipping and sliding, oh what a fright!
The chill might linger, but I'll hold my own,
With laughter that sparkles like ice in my bone.

Whispers Wrapped in White

In winter's chill, I lost my way,
With snowflakes dancing, oh what a fray!
I built a friend, he looked quite neat,
But tripped on ice and fell on my feet.

I tried to sled down a shiny hill,
But landed in a snowman with a thrill.
Thumbs are frozen, can't grab a snack,
Each puff of breath makes me sound like a quack!

The Winter of My Heart

My heart's encased in layers of frost,
Like a penguin wearing a woolly exhaust.
I slip on ice with a comical flair,
Spinning like ballet, quite unaware!

A snowball fight? I'm ready to roll!
But I'm dodging snowmen—a tricky goal.
I launched one high, and it landed on Ted,
Now he's chasing me, I think I'm dead!

Snow-Covered Bliss

The ground's a canvas, all white and bright,
I make my mark, oh what a sight!
But slipping and sliding gets me in binds,
Maybe winter's fun is just for the minds?

Frosty drinks spill and splatter my face,
I laugh so hard, it's a snowy embrace.
Sunshine glimmers like diamonds on ice,
I'd trade it for warmth—oh, I'm thinking twice!

Chasing Shadows in the Snow

I chase my shadow, think it's a game,
But it eludes me, it's so full of shame!
With every step, I land in a drift,
My snowshoes squeaking—they give me a lift!

Building an igloo seemed like a blast,
But the roof collapsed; I was outclassed.
I peeked out quickly, frozen in time,
With icicles hanging, I called it sublime!

Snowflakes on Silent Streets

Glistening flakes fall like confetti,
While squirrels practice their acrobatics.
Feet jump around, a dance so petty,
Do snowmen feel love, or just bad tactics?

Snowballs fly like spontaneous hugs,
Winter's laughter fills the air with cheer.
Kids shout loudly, while dogs pull tugs,
Joyful chaos, let's give a cheer!

The Chill of Love's Breath

Frosty whispers sneak up my nose,
Playful breezes tickle my toes.
Is that affection or just the cold?
Winter's flirtation, a story retold.

Hats fly high with a gusty jab,
Lovers circle, in snowy attire.
Hot cocoa cups and a swipe on the slab,
A snowball fight ignites the fire!

Heartbeats Beneath the Drifts

Beneath thick quilts of white, we dwell,
A cartoon slip on icy paths, oh well!
Giggles explode with each little fall,
In this frosty playground, we've conquered it all.

Warm scarfs knot us with laughter tight,
Each frosty breath, a clouded delight.
Who knew winter could tickle so sweet?
With snowball hugs, it's a thrilling feat!

Shimmering Solitude

In the stillness, each flake is a joke,
The trees hold secrets, like a wise old bloke.
Snowshoes squeak, a whimsical sound,
Nature's giggle in the snowy ground.

A lone penguin waddles, in search of a mate,
He slips and slides, what a comedic fate!
In this frosty stage, joy takes its cue,
Where the fun in the chill, feels fresh and new.

Frozen Whispers

In a land where snowflakes jest,
A snowman wears a scarf, he's blessed.
His carrot nose is quite absurd,
With jokes and puns that fly like birds.

The winter winds, they laugh and play,
While icy critters dance all day.
A frosty cat with paws like cream,
Chases snowflakes in a dream.

Winter's Embrace

In the chill where snowmen smirk,
A squirrel steals a snowflake T-shirt.
Snowball fights with laughter ring,
As penguins slide, oh what a fling!

A frosty breeze whispers in jest,
While mittened hands are warmly pressed.
In winter's hold, the giggles flow,
With hot cocoa, we steal the show!

Echoes of the Frost

Frosty echoes bounce around,
Where snowflakes giggle on the ground.
A rabbit hops with winter flair,
Wearing sunglasses, quite debonair.

The snowman's grin, it's hard to miss,
He's got a snowball aimed for bliss.
In his icy realm, the fun's no bore,
A flurry of laughter—who could ask for more?

Icy Veins

In icy veins, the chuckles flow,
Where penguins waddle to and fro.
A snowflake sneezes, bless its soul,
A frosty giggle, a winter goal.

With snowshoes on, we trip and slide,
While fluffy ducks make quite a glide.
In a winter wonderland so bright,
The frozen fun is pure delight!

Gentle Dreams

With gentle dreams on snowy nights,
Snowmen chat about their flights.
They wish for hats that float and sway,
While giggling through the frosty play.

The stars above look down and grin,
As snowy smiles stretch cheek to chin.
In this land of winter's cheer,
The jokes keep rolling—loud and clear!

Elysium of Snow

In a land where snowmen dance,
With carrots for noses, they prance.
They throw snowballs with glee,
Laughing wild and carefree.

Puddles form as they stomp,
Countless snowflakes start to clomp.
Sleds fly by in a hurry,
Chasing down the winter furry.

The chill asks for cocoa warm,
To wrap us in its cozy charm.
Yet here comes a snowball fight,
Who's winning? It's hard to cite!

As night falls, the snowmen wiggle,
A snow machine starts to giggle.
In this land, we find delight,
Elysium of snow, pure and bright.

Moonlit Frost

Underneath the silver glow,
Snowflakes twirl and put on a show.
A snow cat leaps with a cheer,
Saying, 'Winter is finally here!'

The moon plays peek-a-boo with frost,
Countless dreams of fun embossed.
A penguin slips and starts to slide,
On a sled that couldn't hide!

There's laughter in the chilly air,
As snowmen don their finest wear.
A carrot fights off a hungry crow,
But the crow just wants more snow!

As the sun begins to rise,
Snowmen melt with silly sighs.
Yet with every flake that falls,
Moonlit frost still brings its calls.

The Solace of Ice

In a world where snowflakes cling,
Cocoa cups are the real king.
Winter sprinkles joy like sprout,
While snowflakes swirl and twist about.

Ice skaters spin on frozen lakes,
While a snow hare shares its cakes.
They giggle at penguins that slip,
Falling into a frosty dip!

The sun peeks out, "What's this fun?"
Snowball battles have just begun.
With snowmen raising their glass,
To toast the fun as moments pass!

In this place, smiles take the prize,
As we watch the snowflakes rise.
The ice holds secrets, whispers tight,
In solace, we find pure delight.

Glacial Heartbeat

In the chill where laughter sprawls,
Snowflakes dance and catch our falls.
A winter stroll, feet so light,
Watching icicles drip through night.

Sleds collide with joyful thuds,
Laughter echoes through the buds.
Snowmen's hats blown by the breeze,
Wobbling like their jolly knees!

"Oh dear, are you alright?" I call,
A snowball flies — it's quite the brawl!
In the cold, our spirits bloom,
Snow days chase away the gloom.

As the evening gently glows,
With snowflakes tumbling like prose.
A glacial heartbeat warms the night,
In frozen wonder, all feels right.

Enchanted Snowfall

Frosty flakes in a swirling dance,
Snowmen grinning in a jolly stance.
Sleds are flying, laughter fills the air,
Frosty breath in a chilly flair.

Hot cocoa spills on a cold white floor,
Marshmallows dive, oh what a score!
Snowball fights with a friendly glee,
Laughter echoes, just you and me.

Icicles hanging like crystal swords,
While frozen toes give the loudest chords.
Yet in the fun, here's the twist, you see,
We all slip and fall, quite gracefully!

So let's embrace this winter's charm,
With funny slips that cause no harm.
As snowflakes twirl in a gleeful way,
We laugh and cheer through the frosty play.

Cryogenic Dreams

Chilling nights in a fluff-filled haze,
Dreams of snowmen on snowy bays.
Elves on branches, they're taking aim,
With snowball cannons, it's quite the game.

Waking up with frost on my nose,
Pajamas frozen, oh how it shows!
The ice cream truck has turned to ice,
It's winter madness, isn't this nice?

Slipping past a tree, I fear the crash,
But landing softly? An epic splash!
The snow makes fun of my graceful fall,
Laughter rings out, it's a winter ball.

So here we are in this frozen scheme,
Dancing through life, it's a snowy dream.
Though icy winds may raise a pout,
We'll find the giggles without a doubt.

Heartbeats in the Snow

In the stillness, a thump, a bump,
Snowflakes giggle as they gentle thump.
We stomp through drifts, our boots so bright,
Creating paths in the soft moonlight.

A snowman with a carrot nose stands tall,
But watch out for that sneaky snowball!
With each toss, laughter takes flight,
As we shiver and shake in the frosty night.

Fingers numb but spirits aglow,
Chasing each other through the soft, white flow.
Falling into snow, it's a giggling spree,
"Hey, look! I'm a snow angel!" says she.

So we dance in the cold, our joy the glow,
Warmed by laughter in the winter show.
With icy hearts and warm, bright grins,
We find the fun where the snow begins.

Glimmering Chill

Stars twinkle down with a frosty wink,
Snowflakes cascade as we brave the brink.
Swirling snow makes the world so bright,
While frostbite sneaks in on winter nights.

Jingle bells play in the crisp, cold air,
As snow-covered folks do a funny stare.
With haphazard steps, we glide and slide,
Trying our best to take it in stride.

Mittens on hands but hats askew,
With frozen noses, we bid adieu.
The snowflakes chuckle with a twirling froth,
As winter's mischief brings endless troth.

Under the moon's shining, glowing thrill,
Let's embrace the cold, the glimmering chill.
With laughter ringing in the midnight hue,
We'll dance through the snow, just us two.

The Fragility of Icebound Affection

On winter days, my love runs cold,
My warmth is lost, if truth be told.
We cuddle up, but then we slide,
On frosty floors, we take a ride.

Our laughter echoes, frozen air,
With snowball fights, love's a real dare.
But when you slip and fall, oh dear,
I swear I saw you shed a tear.

Hot cocoa spills, and so do dreams,
We melt away, or so it seems.
Yet winter's chill can't freeze the fun,
In every slip, we're still as one.

So grab a scarf, let's bundle tight,
And dance around, all day and night.
With snowmen tall, and giggles bright,
This frosty love feels just so right.

Glacial Moments

The snowflakes fall, like whispered jokes,
We make a fort, bring out the pokes.
You throw a snowball, I take a dive,
In this winter world, we come alive.

Ice cream cones in winter's grasp,
We lick them fast; oh, what a gasp!
Your nose is red, your cheeks a glow,
We laugh at how your eyebrows snow.

A sledding trip goes off the rails,
We tumble down, the laughter sails.
In icy hugs, we slip and slip,
Our hearts are warm, though icy grip.

So let it freeze, the love we share,
With frosty puns and frigid flair.
Though temperatures might drop to low,
We chill together, and that's the show.

Heartstrings in a Winter Landscape

In winter's chill, we stroll so free,
With matching hats, just you and me.
A snowman chat, with carrot nose,
He listens close, through winter's prose.

A frosty kiss, your lips turn blue,
But laughter reigns, and warmth breaks through.
We frolick in this winter scheme,
Playing tag in a snowy dream.

But when we slip on ice so slick,
Your flailing arms, a funny trick.
We land with grace, like falling leaves,
In winter's dance, love never grieves.

So take my hand, let's twirl and spin,
In this white world, we wear a grin.
With every slip and silly fall,
Our hearts find joy, they stand so tall.

Crystalized Longing

The frozen pond, our secret spot,
You bring the snacks, I bring the plot.
We skate around, but oh, the flips,
We laugh so hard, it's winter's quips.

In crystal snow, we write our names,
Our hearts are part of winter games.
With mittened hands and frozen toes,
We sing our songs, each one a rose.

A flurry starts, we build and throw,
The biggest snowball, steal the show.
But when it lands upon your head,
You're quite the sight in white and red.

So as the frost begins to creep,
We hold on tight, our love to keep.
In every laugh, we find a way,
To warm the coldest winter day.

Cold Caresses

Chilled embraces touch my cheek,
As winter's breath gives me a peek.
I slip and slide on icy ground,
Laughing at my clumsy sound.

Snowflakes fall, a silly dance,
One lands right in my hot cocoa chance.
With marshmallows floating like little boats,
I sip and smile, forgetting my woes.

Noses red from frosty kisses,
Winter makes us all its misses.
We giggle as we stumble, trip,
On frozen paths, oh what a slip!

Icicles hang like teeth of frost,
Mouths agape, in laughter lost.
In this chilly world we find,
Warm hearts, though snowflakes blind.

White Lies of Winter

In a fluff of white, I try to hide,
With snow as my trusty, cold ally.
I tell the trees, 'I'm not that cold,'
While shivering beneath their hold.

Snowmen grin with carrot noses,
But melt away like secret foes-es.
I whisper to them, 'Stay for tea!'
They wink and giggle; they just can't be.

While building forts, we cast soft shouts,
'Get in, get in! Watch out for routes!'
Snowball fights that lead to hugs,
Winter's tricks are so warm and snug.

With every slip and silly fall,
Laughter echoes, we have a ball.
Winter's white lies, all in fun,
Who cares if we can't find the sun?

Frosted Serenity

In the quiet of frozen nights,
Winter whispers, 'Join the sights.'
I trip on snow, and oh, what grace,
The ground calls, 'Come join the race!'

Frosty bushes wear a gleam,
While I chase a snowball dream.
Down the hill, I tumble free,
Like a boulder, oh, woe is me!

Serenity wrapped in frosty gleam,
While snowflakes tease like a happy dream.
Rabbits dance in velvet white,
As I laugh at winter's bite.

In twinkling light, the streetlamps glow,
But here in the chaos, I take my bow.
For winter's charm pulls me in,
With frosted fun, let games begin!

Beneath the Snowy Veil

Beneath a quilt of fluffy white,
I sneak around with sheer delight.
Snowballs ready in a playful hand,
I dodge, I duck, this isn't planned!

The trees stand tall like silent guards,
As I prepare, oh, my backyard!
With laughter loud, I make my stand,
In this frosty wonderland.

Hot chocolate waits with whipped cream dollops,
In winter's grip, we pop like lollipops.
Sipping slowly, my cheeks aglow,
What winter tricks will next unfold?

Beneath each flake, a giggle lies,
Surprises lurking, oh, what a prize!
In snowy laughter, our hearts conspire,
A warmth in cold that won't expire.

Shimmering Chill

In a coat that's two sizes too big,
I waddle like a penguin, oh so big!
Snowflakes tickle my nose, what a sight,
I sneeze and start a snowball fight!

Penguins slide and have tons of fun,
While I slip on ice, oh what a run!
Chasing my hat in the winter breeze,
While squirrels giggle up in the trees!

With cocoa in hand, I dream of heat,
But find my snowman with two left feet!
He's got a carrot that's seen better days,
He's a fashion icon in all the wrong ways!

So let's build castles till springtime's call,
Laughter echoes as we tumble and fall!
With every chill, my jokes seem to grow,
I'm a stand-up comic in a winter show!

Frozen Reverie

In a land where snowmen wear funny hats,
I dance with deer and chatter with bats!
Wolves howl tunes of absurd delight,
While I trip on ice, oh what a sight!

Snowflakes giggle as they fall down,
My nose turns red; I'm the talk of the town!
Caught in a snowdrift, I lose my way,
A snowball flies in; oh, what a play!

With cheeks so rosy and laughter so bright,
I take on the winter with all of my might!
There's warmth in my heart, though fingers are cold,
A fool in the snow, so silly, so bold!

So let's twirl and slide on this frosty stage,
As snowflakes create our own winter page!
My frozen thoughts warm up with each cheer,
For in this blizzard, it's fun we hold dear!

Winter's Caress

Bundle up tight in my puffy attire,
I resemble a marshmallow, I must inspire!
Frosty whispers make my lips go blue,
I try to whistle, but it sounds like a moo!

Snowball battles, a flurry of glee,
The neighbor's cat looks baffled at me!
I throw a snowball, it hits my own head,
Now I giggle in my snowy bed!

Hot chocolate spills while I dance in the fray,
That sip of warmth leads me astray!
I chase my dog, but he's slippery fast,
We tumble together—what a comical blast!

Winter's grip brings wild, silly times,
Snowmen adorned with mismatched chimes!
So let's celebrate, laughing without shame,
In this frosty wonder, we're all a bit lame!

Crystalized Longing

In a world where icicles grow on my nose,
I dream of summer while my frozen toes doze!
Every step I take, I slip and slide,
Snowflakes pirouette, happy to glide!

My snowman grins with a crooked smile,
He's stolen my scarf, oh what a trial!
I try to reclaim it, my balance is off,
We both end up laughing, unable to scoff!

Winter's frosty chill tickles my ear,
My laughter echoes; there's nothing to fear!
With friends all around, snowballs take flight,
Who knew frozen fun could feel so right?

Though the world outside looks harsh and gray,
I find joy among the snow where I play!
In a whimsical dance, we leap and we swing,
Together we cherish this winter's zing!

Shards of Frozen Time

In winter's grasp, I lost my shoe,
It slipped away, right past a loo.
The snowmen laugh, they know this game,
I chase my foot, yet feel no shame.

My scarf's a noodle, flapping free,
It dances 'round like it's got glee.
I trip on ice, I glide with style,
The frozen ground is now my tile.

With hot cocoa, I make a mess,
Whipped cream mustache, I must confess.
Each sip a giggle, each sip a grin,
My winter joy is sparked within.

So gather 'round, some friends in tow,
We'll find our laughter in the snow.
With every slip, a tale we weave,
In frozen fun, we all believe.

Enchanted by the Cold

The snowflakes tinkle like tiny bells,
They swirl and dance, casting their spells.
A penguin waddles, gives a wink,
On frozen ponds, I start to sink.

My nose is red, like Rudolph's glow,
To catch this chill, I must bestow.
A snowball fight turns into laughs,
We're all just kids on wintry paths.

Hot chocolate mugs, they clink and cheer,
Whipped cream mountains are never sheer.
With marshmallow snowmen, we craft delight,
In this brisk air, we take flight.

As frost wraps all in sparkling sheen,
My goofy grin can rarely be seen.
Yet in this cold, we find our heat,
With frosty fun, life is sweet.

Love's Frosty Reflection

Oh love is grand in icy realms,
Yet watch your step, it overwhelms.
I slipped on ice, fell right on cue,
A heart that thumps, and then it flew.

You threw a snowball, but it missed,
Instead, it hit a tree—how twist!
Laughter echoes through snowy nights,
As we frolic in these chilly lights.

Your frozen breath, it dances bright,
Like little clouds in the moonlight.
But when we cuddle, oh what a sight,
Two snowflakes lost, yet feeling right.

With mittens on, we grip so tight,
Amid the cold, our hearts ignite.
In every slip, we play our part,
Building joy that won't depart.

Petals Beneath the Powder

Beneath the snow, I found a rose,
Its petals soft, in ice they froze.
I leaned to sniff, got snow in nose,
Ah, winter's gift, how it glows.

The garden's dressed in frosty white,
I brought some bread for a snowball fight.
Squirrels watch, their cheeks all stuffed,
While I throw fluff, they look quite huffed.

Yet through this chill, we warm the air,
With puns and giggles, joy we share.
Let's build a fort and claim this ground,
In laughter's echo, love is found.

So raise your cup, let's toast the cold,
For in this freeze, our hearts are bold.
With petals lost, we chase the fun,
In every snowflake, we are one.

Life Underneath the Snow

Beneath the layer, soft and bright,
A squirrel slips, what a funny sight!
He thinks he's flying, doing a spin,
But oh dear friend, that's not how to win.

Snowmen wobbled, their buttons askew,
One loses an arm; oh, not another too!
They chuckle and sway, in a chilly dance,
This winter's breeze gives a silly chance.

All the snowflakes drift like dreams,
In mittens, they snicker as giggle-teams.
A sledding race with giggles galore,
While snowballs fly - oh, here comes more!

With every flake that falls from the sky,
A little frosty mischief goes by.
The world's a stage wrapped in white,
Let's laugh together till the morning light.

Winter's Tender Touch

A snowball fight breaks out in delight,
With laughter echoing into the night.
But who's the target? It's a comedy show,
When snowballs miss, and the laughter flows!

Carrot noses on snow-folk smile wide,
One lost its hat in a breezy glide.
They shake off the snow like cats in the sun,
Wobbling around, just having some fun.

The trees wear coats, all fluffy and neat,
Icicles dangle, quite the icy treat.
A twig snaps loudly, we jump with a start,
Winter's touch is silly, and it warms the heart.

Chasing a puppy who leaps with such glee,
Tumbles and rolls in snow, oh, carefree!
With frosty noses and rosy cheeks,
Join the laughter of winter's peaks!

Heart Wrapped in White

A fluffy blanket drapes upon the ground,
Where snowmen joke and silliness abounds.
Two little kids with big, goofy grins,
Constructing a fortress, where laughter begins.

Snowflakes fall like little chuckles of cheer,
Dancing and twirling, they've nothing to fear.
One lands on a tongue, what a frosty surprise,
To catch winter's giggles right under the skies.

Ice skaters slip, on a pond made of glass,
With spins and tumbles, oh, what a class!
Laughter erupts with every tiny fall,
Each frosty encounter becomes a new call.

All bundled up, while sipping hot treats,
The world is a playground on snow-covered sheets.
With giggles and warmth, let's embrace the cold,
For this whimsical joy never gets old!

Imprints in the Frost

Little footprints dance in a wiggly line,
Chasing the dog who's crossing divine.
He leaps like a rocket, so full of delight,
Leaving us laughing in the bright winter light.

Snowflakes plotting in a magical scheme,
Whispers of warmth in a frosty dream.
While snowmen grumble, losing their hats,
A frosty wind comes, and oh, how it chats!

Frosty windows are masterpieces bright,
Framed with a laugh, no need for a fight.
The world is a canvas, coasting in cheer,
With each chilly giggle that brings winter near.

As the twilight descends on a snowy white scene,
Snow-ballers unite in a playful routine.
So here's to the laughter, the joy that it brings,
In a world draped in frost, where the fun never ends.

Snowbound Solitude

In winter's grip, I found my peace,
As snowflakes dance, my cares release.
But every step I take, I slip,
On icy paths, just like a trip.

The birdies hop with fuzzy socks,
While squirrels wear their winter frocks.
I wave at snowmen, proud and tall,
Who've got it all, not me at all!

Together we toast with cocoa steams,
While snowball fights disrupt my dreams.
I build a fort, my snowy lair,
Then lose the battle—oh, despair!

Yet in this chill, a warmth I find,
Among the flurries, peace of mind.
For in each drift, I laugh and play,
As frosty friends come out to stay.

Chilled Affection

Oh, winter whispers through the trees,
With frosty breath that makes me sneeze.
I bundled up, looking quite round,
Like a marshmallow, oh so profound!

The snowflakes tickle my rosy nose,
As I waddle through the icy prose.
With mittens on, I wave to friends,
While inner laughter never ends.

Hot chocolate spills as I take a sip,
I laugh and spill—oh, bless this trip!
The snowman grins with a carrot smile,
He knows my secrets; he stays awhile.

But in this chill, connections bloom,
Like frosty flowers in the gloom.
We'll dance in boots with frozen toes,
And share our warmth beneath snows.

Glacial Echoes

The echoes of laughter fill the air,
As we slip and slide without a care.
A frozen cheer spills everywhere,
While tumbling snowballs turn to flair!

I try to skate on icy ponds,
But end up making silly bonds.
With every scoot and goofy spin,
I look like I'm on a bumpy win!

The snowflakes chime in harmony,
As I miss the ground and fall with glee.
With snow-flecked cheeks, I laugh aloud,
My frosty heart is feeling proud!

Each icy hug brings joy anew,
With frozen friends and cocoa too.
In glacial cheer, we're never alone,
Together we warm this frosty throne.

Whispered Frost

In whispers soft, the frost does creep,
As I tumble down, still half asleep.
The snowflakes giggle as I land,
With cheeks like apples—puffing grand.

Wearing scarves like enormous boas,
I look like a fashionista, oh, yes, it shows!
My winter coat is two sizes too big,
I waddle like a penguin, doing a jig!

I sip on soup that's way too hot,
My tongue's a casualty, oh what a plot!
With frosty bubbles in my nose,
I laugh out loud—everyone knows!

Yet as I roam this winter land,
With snowy wonder all unplanned,
I find that joy's within this frost,
In chuckles shared, we are not lost.

Flurries of Emotion

In winter's grip, I slipped and fell,
My feelings scattered, can't you tell?
With icy patches and frosty cheer,
I laugh and wobble, shed a tear.

Snowflakes tickle, they dance and play,
My joy escapes in a snowy ballet.
Slipping and sliding, oh what a sight,
Who knew chill could spark such delight?

When winter's jests bring laughter near,
I find solace in grins, not fear.
For every cold shiver, a giggle is found,
Frosty frolics and joy abound!

A snowman grinning, my old pal too,
We share silly secrets, a funny view.
Chasing winter's laughs, it feels so good,
At the end of the day, it's all understood!

Heartstrings in the Frost

Cold fingers poke, who told them to play?
They tug on my heartstrings in a chilly way.
I shuffle about in my big winter coat,
Can't feel my toes, but hey, isn't it a hoot?

Snowballs whizz past, a war declaration,
In the frosty field, oh what a sensation!
Tom and I clash, with laughter we shout,
Who knew cold days could turn us about?

Frosted trees with branches so wide,
I climbed one once, thought it a ride.
But down I came with a thump and a slide,
Guess winter's humor is hard to abide!

In this frosty realm, we're all a bit jolly,
As we fumble for warmth in our grand ol' folly.
With laughter as bright as the morning sun,
I polish my skates, let the fun times run!

The Silent Thaw

Winter whispers, then giggles aloud,
A thawing heart beneath a frosty shroud.
As ice cubes clink in my cup of tea,
I ponder how wild and free I can be!

A melted snowman droops, what a tale!
His carrot nose? Oh dear, it's gone pale.
With puddles around and splashes to make,
I dance in the rain, for goodness' sake!

Frosty mornings give way to warm sun,
I'm tripping on laughter and having such fun.
The winter is sly, but I'll win this round,
With sunshine at last, joy well-found!

So raise a glass filled with ice and cheer,
To melting emotions, the end of the year.
For even in cold, love's warmth remains,
With each giggle, I lose my chains!

Ethereal Melodies

In a frosty world, we sing our song,
Melodies chirp, not a moment feels wrong.
Snowflakes fall like confetti from skies,
Each laugh a note that floats and flies.

Caroling with chattering teeth, what a scene!
I belt out tunes, like a snow-covered queen.
A wintry twist on an old, merry tune,
As I dance through the drifts, beneath the moon.

The air holds a magic, sparkling and bright,
Where thoughts turn to snow, like fluffy delight.
With frozen fingers, I wave a grand night,
In this surreal land, everything feels right!

So twirl in the snow, let giggles take flight,
In a waltz with winter, oh what a sight!
For here in this wonder, we're young, not old,
At the edge of the universe, icy tales unfold!

The Shiver Within

In winter's chill, I dance around,
My toes are frozen underground.
I dress in layers, feel so spry,
Yet still I shiver, oh my, oh my!

A snowball fights a friendly foe,
But why's my nose the color of snow?
With frosty breath, I start to laugh,
And trip on ice—what a silly gaffe!

I try to sled, to glide with grace,
But end up stuck in a snowy place.
My cheeks are red, my hair a mess,
Oh winter fun, you bring such stress!

So here I am, with frostbit pride,
A comic winter, I can't hide.
I'll make a snowman, round and bright,
And hope it doesn't start a snowball fight!

Silent Winter Echoes

The winter winds do softly blow,
And tickle my nose like a jabbering crow.
I slip and slide on icy ground,
While squirrels laugh, oh what a sound!

Snowflakes fall like a clumsy dance,
My mittens fly, I can't take a chance.
With every puff, my breath turns white,
I'm an icy dragon, bringing delight!

I build a fort, oh what a sight,
A fortress tall to win the fight.
But in the end, my friends all swarm,
And soon it's chaos—what a warm!

So here I stand, a snowball king,
A funny sight, I laugh and sing.
With frosty cheeks, I can't deny,
Winter makes me giggle, oh my, oh my!

Snowy Reveries

I woke up to a world of white,
With snowflakes falling, oh what a sight!
I donned my coat, stepped out with glee,
And promptly fell—oh, woe is me!

A snowman grows with carrots bright,
But its arms are wobbly, what a fright!
I offer it a hat of red,
It falls right off, oh what a head!

While snowflakes dance upon my nose,
The winter wind plays peek-a-boos.
I wave to kids on tiny sleds,
They're speeding past while I lose my threads!

With hot cocoa to warm my toes,
I laugh at all my winter woes.
Oh snowy days, you bring such cheer,
Amidst the giggles, winter's here!

Frosted Memories

In the frost, I start to seek,
A pair of gloves—oh, what a cheek!
One's here, the other's gone,
It must have frolicked on its own!

The icicles drip like frozen tears,
I slip and slide—oh dear, oh dear!
I wave to neighbors from icy caves,
They wave back with frosty waves!

Snowball battles bring lots of laughs,
But I get hit—what wicked gaffs!
With cheeks like cherries, I chase and run,
'Neath falling flakes, we have such fun!

So here's to winter, full of cheer,
With all its antics, it's my favorite year.
In frosty moments, we find delight,
As we giggle at our winter fight!

Ethereal Snowdrift

In winter's chill, my nose turns bright,
I tripped on snow, oh what a sight!
With every step, a crunch and a crack,
My boots are villains, they always attack.

Snowballs fly like bullets in flight,
Just missed my hat, oh what a fright!
Laughter rolls like snow down the hill,
Where frosty fun gives the heart a thrill.

A snowman grins, his buttons askew,
With a carrot nose, he bids me adieu!
I wave goodbye to my icy foe,
As he melts away, all in a row.

But in my dreams, snowflakes dance light,
Tickling my cheeks, oh what a delight!
Winter may freeze, but it also brings cheer,
In the land of snow, I disappear!

Heart of the Winter Sky

The clouds above are fluffy and round,
They whisper secrets without a sound.
I tried to catch one, but slipped with a squeal,
Landed in snow, what a cold ordeal!

Snowmen are laughing, they've had too much fun,
With a hat on their head, they all think they've won.
I tossed them a snowball, they tumbled so free,
Who knew winter was such a comedy?

I slip on ice, do a little dance,
Look at my friends, they're lost in a trance.
Their faces turn red, they're laughing so hard,
I'm the winter clown, always on guard!

With snowflakes falling like sprinkles from sky,
I catch them on tongues, oh my, oh my!
Nature's confetti, embracing the glow,
Every giggle a sparkle, wrapped in fresh snow.

Solstice Serenade

At the stroke of dawn, the world glimmers white,
I step out my door, oh what a sight!
Snowflakes tango, they twirl and they spin,
But my frozen fingers say this can't win.

My sled's ready, gives me a boast,
I'm off down the slope, I'm going to coast!
But a bump and a tumble, oh what a race,
I'm now the king of the snowy disgrace!

The snow's getting thicker, I'm searching for joy,
Might find it outside, or in a toy.
But wait, what's that? A snowflake on me,
It tickles my cheek, it demands to be free!

So I sing to the winter, with a chuckle and cheer,
While the snowflakes gather, oh come bring me beer!
Laughter wrapped up in a frosty embrace,
In winter's great ballroom, we dance with grace.

Faded Footprints

A path is made through snowdrifts high,
With footprints left for birds to spy.
I follow my trail, with hopes I won't stray,
But a snowbank beckons, and leads me astray!

The chubby squirrel gives me a glance,
It scampers away, missing my chance.
I take a step, then slide and I spin,
Winter wonderland's your crazy kin!

The snow whispers secrets, it giggles tonight,
As I tumble and laugh, oh what a sight!
With mittens all soggy and cheeks rosy red,
I'm a snowstorm's jester, in whirlwinds I tread.

So here's to the snow that makes us all glee,
Creating the joys that warm hearts like tea.
In the shuffle and shuffle of soft winter cheer,
I find my true magic, let's laugh through the year!

Shivering Whispers

I tried to make a snowman, oh what a sight,
But he looked like my uncle after too much ice at night.
With a carrot for a nose and stones for his grin,
He waved at the kids like he owned the spin.

A snowball fight erupted, laughter in the air,
But my aim was so bad, I hit my friend's hair.
They squealed and they laughed, I blushed and turned red,

Next time I'll stick to snowflakes instead.

Oh look at that snow, it's soft and it's bright,
But I tripped on a patch and fell out of sight.
They buried me softly; snow piled on my toes,
I laughed as they dug me, "I just wanted to pose!"

The winter's a joker, it's playing its game,
Making me feel like a clumsy old lame.
So here's to the fun, in every cold slip,
Let's dance through the snow like we're on a big trip!

The Lullaby of Winter

Frosty the friend sat by the door,
Napping and snoring, what a furry bore!
I tossed him a snowball, hit him right on the head,
He jumped up surprised, "Do you want me for bread?"

The flakes fell like feathers, light as a breeze,
I danced like a penguin, trying to tease.
But I slipped and I flopped, oh what a display,
Now I'm the joke of winter's ballet!

Hot cocoa in hand, it's steaming for sure,
But it slipped from my grip, who could want more?
It splashed on my lap, I leapt up with glee,
"Winter wonders are magic, just look at me!"

So here's to the chill, with laughter abound,
Let's shred through the snow with our giggles all around.
In this jolly old frost, let's conquer the cold,
With chuckles and snowmen, tales to be told!

Echoes Beneath the Frost

Beneath the white cover, secrets do hide,
A squirrel with a hat thinks it's fashion, not pride.
He chattered and scolded, yet struck quite a pose,
While I chuckled and fell on my nose!

Icicles dangling, sharp as a knife,
I challenged my friends: 'Let's play winter strife!'
But slip after slip, we lay on the ground,
With laughter and giggles, winter wrap-around.

Snow forts were built, all shapes and all sizes,
But mine looked like pudding, with tons of surprises.
Then came the snowplow, rude in its haste,
My masterpiece gone, not a trace left to taste!

Yet winter's a jest, with stories to weave,
To the frosty old winds, we chuckle and cleave.
So let's spin and twirl through this chilly delight,
For what's life without laughter in the frosty night?

Melodies of the Falling Snow

The snowflakes are singing, a soft, chilly song,
But I'm tripping and falling, what could go wrong?
With laughter around, I try to keep pace,
Only to slip, and fall flat on my face!

A snow angel made, I flapped like a fish,
But it ended up looking like a wintery dish.
The kids gathered 'round with giggles galore,
"Is it a bird?" "No, it's a snow who fell poor!"

With mittens like boats, our hands feel so cold,
We tossed snow at targets, or so I was told.
But my aim went awry, hit the neighbor's fine car,
Now I'm dodging from winter, just like a shy star!

So here's to the snow and the warmth of this cheer,
Let's frost up our hearts and pour laughter like beer.
In the chill of the night, let's embrace every swirl,
For life is a laugh when you give it a twirl!

The Chill of yesteryear

Once I made a snowman, it looked quite tall,
But it melted in laughter, a puddle, oh what a fall!
With a carrot for a nose, it gave me a wink,
Then slipped on ice, made me giggle, I think!

Every winter's a chance for new frosty fun,
But last year's snowball fight? It's still on the run!
With snowballs like cannonballs, we took our stance,
But all we did was slip, oh how we danced!

The chilly breeze told secrets, I heard it say,
"Winter's just nature's way of making us play!"
So I donned my mittens and danced 'til the night,
Tripping over snowdrifts, what a silly sight!

So here's to the winters, both wacky and wild,
Where frost bites our noses, like a mischievous child!
Each snowflake like laughter that sparkles and glows,
In the chill of yesteryear, anything goes!

Beneath the Frosty Veil

Beneath the frosty cover, all sparkly and white,
I stumbled on a snowdrift, gave a little fright!
With a hop and a tumble, I found myself prone,
A snow angel I made, but my wings were all blown!

The squirrels in their jackets, they laughed at my fall,
As I landed with style, no grace at all!
They chattered up a storm, critiquing my flair,
With tiny paws clapping, they gave me their stare.

Every snowflake that dances, has a giggle or two,
They twirl like they're laughing, enchanting the view!
I tried to catch one, it tickled my nose,
And off it went, laughing, as the winter wind blows!

So here's to the winter, the giggles, the cheer,
Beneath this frosty veil, there's nothing to fear!
Let's build our snow castles, with laughter and grace,
In this silly winter wonderland, we'll find our place!

Winter's Heartbeat

Winter's heartbeat echoes, as the chill settles down,
With icicles like trumpets, making me frown!
I stepped out this morning, my feet cold as stone,
But the snowflakes just laughed, I wasn't alone!

Each puff of white air makes me giggle out loud,
While I trip over snowmen, they're terribly proud!
They grin with their buttons, like they just stole the show,

While I'm stuck in a snowdrift like a marshmallow!

The trees wear their blankets, all frosty and bright,
They're whispering secrets throughout the long night!
I'm bundled in layers, looking silly and wide,
As the snowflakes keep swirling, giggling, they glide.

So let's dance with the winter, and celebrate glee,
With snow angels and snowballs, just you wait and see!
With every frosty heartbeat, we'll laugh through the chill,

In this wonder of winter, our hearts will be filled!

Whispering Snowflakes

Whispering snowflakes are gossiping near,
They chuckle and tumble, oh what a cheer!
With each little flake, there's a giggle or jest,
Forming cozy snow people, looking quite blessed!

I attempted to sled, oh what a grand sight,
But I zoomed past the hill, what a comical flight!
The snowman just chuckled, with a grin big and round,
"Next time, dear friend, try to slow down!"

The penguins in the park, they're plotting their scheme,
To make a snowball army, it's more of a dream!
With a flurry of feathers, they plan to attack,
But they slip on their own, "Let's just grab a snack!"

So here in the winter, where laughter runs free,
The snowflakes keep dancing, just you wait and see!
With a sprinkle of fun, they blanket the night,
In this whimsical winter, everything's bright!

Frost-Laden Confessions

I once tried to dance on ice,
But slipped right into snowman's slice.
His carrot nose gave me a poke,
I fell and laughed — what a joke!

Chillin' tea with icy flair,
My friend declared, "It's quite rare!"
Check your cup for frostbite, mate,
Or the cocoa could just wait!

The snowflakes giggled as they fell,
Each landing softly, casting a spell.
I caught a few on my tongue so quick,
They froze, dissolved — a magic trick!

My heart was bright, a snowball true,
With frosty thoughts, I'd start anew.
But every time I tried to throw,
I'd ended up in piles of snow!

The Wintering Heart

In winter's clutch, my warmth takes flight,
Yet I dress up like a marshmallow white.
With layers thick and laughter cold,
I dance around, feeling quite bold.

Snowy antics busting my seams,
Snowball fights fuel the wildest dreams.
But watch your back, or your face will have
A frosty kiss from my playful jab!

Riding sleds down a hill with glee,
I crashed into a tree—who knew me?
The laughter erupted, my pride did thaw,
Big smiles and giggles, a punk-rock flaw!

A snowman's hat, a squirrel's disdain,
They tease me, but I can't complain.
For winter's embrace is a jolly affair,
With every chuckle, joy fills the air!

Secrets Beneath the Ice

Under the ice, there's a secret flow,
Where penguins sing and the snowflakes glow.
They gossip about the clumsy ones,
Like me, who's fallen for winter's puns!

Hiding beneath all that fluffy white,
A secret club meets under moonlight.
Snowmen trade tales of their chilly feats,
While we enjoy hot cocoa and sweet treats.

I found a snowflake that whispered my name,
It giggled at my ungraceful aim.
With a flick and a swirl, it flew from my hand,
And crashed right into a snowdrift band!

Winter's laughter fills the chilly air,
With secrets and smiles, I'm free from care.
Each snowy adventure, a funny delight,
In this frosty world, my heart feels light!

Cold Reverberations

My heart beats like a snow globe spun,
It twirls and whirls, oh what fun!
With chilly thrills and giggles galore,
When winter's song is at my door.

Now please beware — I've got a snowball,
With your name on it? Well, I can't say at all!
But when it flies, you'll surely know,
A love tap straight from winter's bow.

Frosty hair and chilly cheeks,
I'm laughing loud, no time for squeaks.
So shake a leg, don't be so shy,
Join me under the frosty sky!

In the cold, we dance and sing,
Echoing laughter, what joy it brings.
So as the snowflakes fall and play,
We'll warm our hearts in a silly way!

Frozen Yearnings

In a world of ice and cheer,
My toes are cold, oh dear!
I sip hot cocoa with a grin,
While snowflakes flurry on my chin.

The penguins dance, a wobbly sight,
Their tuxedos fit just right.
I join their fun with floppy moves,
While winter's chill my laughter proves.

Snowmen grinning from the street,
With carrot noses, oh so sweet!
But when the sun shows up to play,
I swear they laugh and melt away!

A snowball fight, a frantic spree,
With slippery socks, we trip with glee.
Through frosty air, we dash and glide,
With frozen faces, we can't hide!

Enchantment in White

In a snow globe world so bright,
I lost my mittens, oh what a fright!
The snowflakes twirl, they dance around,
While I keep falling to the ground.

My sled's a rocket, speed of light,
But I spin out, what a sight!
I land in a bush, my cheeks all red,
As giggles echo in my head.

The hills, they call, a siren's song,
My cheeks are numb, but I push along.
Snow angels made, with arms spread wide,
And hot chocolate waits by the fire inside.

A snowman sports a fancy hat,
As my dog tries to chase a cat.
With every laugh, the cold feels slight,
In this winter wonderland tonight!

Shadows of Winter

In shadows deep, where snowflakes churn,
I find myself in quite a turn.
The wind, it whispers silly tales,
Of frozen mittens and frosty flails.

A snowball rolls, a dangerous fate,
That lands it seems on my old mate.
With laughter ringing through the air,
We dodge and weave, a snowy affair.

I tried to build a fort so grand,
But ended up on snow-dusted land.
My friends just snicker, can't hide their glee,
As I wrestle with snow, what's left of me?

Through frosted breath and giggling fits,
In winter's grip, we share our wits.
While shadows dance and snowflakes fall,
We freeze our faces and have a ball!

An Elegy in Ice

Oh icy realm, where laughter's loud,
In meltaway moments, I'm so proud.
A slip and slide, the grace of a swan,
A dance of chaos, my dignity gone.

The frozen pond, it's quite a tease,
Inviting me to skate with ease.
But one misstep, and down I go,
A flailing splash, the world in snow.

My scarf flies off to join the breeze,
As I hope to land with effortless ease.
But winter's grip is far too strong,
And laughter bubbles where I belong.

So raise a toast, with cocoa warm,
To snowy days that bring such charm.
For in this frosty, funny plight,
We live for joy in the winter's bite!

Snowbound Secrets

In frosty coats, we trudge along,
A snowball fight that feels so wrong.
The snowman waves with a carrot nose,
As laughter echoes, and hilarity grows.

Sleds zoom past like rockets on ice,
We've crafted a fort, a snug little slice.
Yet snowflakes fall, like whispers so sly,
'They're plotting!' we giggle, 'Oh my, oh my!'

In winter's grip, we sip hot chocolate,
The marshmallows dance, oh what a pocket!
We toast to the chill with mugs raised high,
While snowflakes swirl like a cheeky pie.

So gather your friends, let mischief fly,
With snowbound secrets that tickle the sky.
Each frosty moment, we'll treasure and share,
In snowy delight, with laughter and flair.

The Embrace of Cold

Wrapped tight in layers, we huddle and squeak,
A penguin parade, wheezing cheek to cheek.
Frostbitten noses and cheeks that glow,
We dance through the snow like it's a cabaret show.

Snowflakes flirt like mischievous sprites,
Tickling our faces in playful bites.
Chasing each other through flurries so bold,
Slipping and sliding, we dance in the cold.

With each frosty breath, our laughter leaps,
As we tumble down hills into fluffy heaps.
"Who's lost a mitten?!" we giggle and cheer,
As snowmen smile, lending a frosty ear.

In the cool embrace where antics unfold,
We find that winter isn't just cold.
With every slip and silly mistake,
We're warmed by the joy that we joyfully make.

Heartbeats in Hibernation

In winter's nest, we snuggle and sway,
While snowflakes settle, let's dance and play.
The world outside is a blanket of white,
But inside, we're warm, giggling with delight.

We'll build igloos and pretend we're bears,
Napping on cushions without a care.
With snacks in tow, the games must commence,
Jokes fly like snowballs, so incredibly dense.

We huddle together, tag-teaming the cold,
As tales of the summer start feeling bold.
"Remember when diving was fun?" Will we dare?
We'll snicker and chuckle, wrapped up in the air.

So while winter wraps its fingers around,
We'll fill up the silence with giggles profound.
For heartbeats may slow in hibernation,
But laughter will thrive as our joyous foundation.

Flickers of Warmth

The fire flickers like a dance gone awry,
While we roast marshmallows and candy to fly.
With chocolate rivers and gooey delight,
We create snowy treats that vanish from sight.

We share stories of winters from days of yore,
While wheels of laughter just roll on the floor.
"Remember that time I slipped on my cake?"
We laugh till we snort, for goodness' sake!

The chill is a prankster, with sneezes galore,
But hot cocoa hugs us and offers us more.
Like snowflakes that twirl, we're light on our feet,
Spreading warmth with our giggles, oh isn't it sweet?

So here's to the frosty yet funny embrace,
The warmth that we share, lights up every space.
In snowy delight and laughter that swells,
We're cozy together, with giggles that dwell.

Liquid Snow

When winter comes that chilly friend,
I slip and slide, around the bend.
My feet do tango, my legs entwine,
With laughter bright, I surely shine.

The snowflakes fall, they look so sweet,
Like little sprinkles on my feet.
I build a snowman, quite a sight,
With a carrot nose and eyes so bright.

But oh, the sun, it shows no care,
Melting dreams, here and there.
I chase the puddles, quite a show,
Slipping back—oh, where'd it go?

Yet in the spring, a warm embrace,
Winter's fun, I still can trace.
With tales of slips, and frosty fun,
Liquid memory of a frozen run.

A Dance with Frost

Frosty mornings, what a sight,
I tiptoe softly, not so bright.
The grass wears crystals, like a coat,
I waltz with trees, they laugh and gloat.

My frozen fingers, what a mess,
I try to catch snowflakes, I confess.
They giggle by, they flurry near,
I spin and twirl—oh dear, oh dear!

A snowball fight, oh what a game,
I hit my friend, but we're not the same.
He rolls and tumbles, what a scream,
We laugh and glide, like in a dream!

The icy dance, it comes to close,
With winter's end, we feel the woes.
Yet memories twirl, and melt away,
In our hearts, they're here to stay.

Encased in Crystal

In a crystal coat, I gleam and shine,
Like a disco ball, I feel divine!
The winter chill, a frosty tease,
Makes sipping cocoa feel like ease.

Icicles hang from the eaves so poised,
With a sharpness that leaves me overjoyed.
I poke at them, they laugh and sway,
Challenging me to come out and play.

Snow forts built, with walls so grand,
Each corner boasts a solid stand.
A snowball barrage, a playful war,
Laughter echoes, what else is in store?

Yet as the sun cracks through the frost,
My fortress melts, oh what a loss!
But memories remain, bright and clear,
Encased in laughter, year after year.

Fragments of Winter

Little shards of ice, they jump and gleam,
In the sun's warm light, they dance and beam.
My nose is red from the frosty bite,
I stumble about, in sparkly delight.

Snowflakes fall, with tricks up their sleeves,
Each one whispers, "Catch me, please!"
I reach for them, they twirl and play,
In their swirling waltz, I lose my way.

Hot cocoa spills as I slide on by,
I laugh out loud, as the mug goes dry.
With marshmallows chasing, a fluffy crew,
Perfect companions for my winter view.

Yet, as the fragments start to fade,
I gather joy from the memories made.
For in every slip and frosty cheer,
Winter's fragments always bring me near.

Milton Keynes UK
Ingram Content Group UK Ltd.
UKHW030751121124
451094UK00013B/790

9 789916 943939